Jan Seale

Valley Ark
Life Along the Rio

Poems by Jan Epton Seale
Photographs by Ansen Seale

KNOWING PRESS

Acknowledgements

Some poems in this book have been published
in *Mesquite Review, riverSedge, Texas Poetry
Calendars 2001, 2002, 2005,* and *The Valley
Land Fund Newsletter,* as well as broadcast
over NPR's *Theme and Variations.* Thanks to Jane
Kittleman for reviewing the content.

ISBN 0-936927-57-7

Printed by Cenveo/Clarke Printing, San Antonio, Texas, USA

The Knowing Press
400 Sycamore
McAllen, TX 78501

Table of Contents

This duet of images and poems grew out of Ansen's and my continuing amazement at the plant and animal life along the Rio. And, admittedly, it was an excuse for a parent and her grown son to find connection in creative play after the passage of time had sent us on our separate ways.

When Ansen was a young child, we lived in an old farmhouse north of McAllen. He and his brothers rode the bus home from Jackson Elementary. They got off at the corner of what is now the intersection of Second and Violet and wandered east through a huge orange grove to reach home.

Sometimes they reported seeing a large black snake slither across their path or a solitary heron standing and staring at them. Once they arrived home with their lunch pails filled with frogs.

Fast forward. One June dawn, when Ansen was seventeen, we drove him to the Brownsville airport to fly away to the island of Sardinia in the Mediterranean for a summer's student visit made possible by the local chapter of the American Field Service.

He was armed with a camera and experience in his McAllen Boy Scout photography troop. Concerned parents of a first-born literally flying from the nest, we were delivering last-minute instructions and admonitions. In the place of reply, we heard Ansen croon, "Oh wow, look at that sunrise!" He was already enamoured of the larger world.

When he came home in late August, he had on film not only certain Sardinian tourist attractions but a conspicuous collection of Italian house cats sitting on walls beside—what else?—bougainvillea.

Ansen has returned again and again to the Valley from his home in San Antonio, always with camera and curiosity about the land he was born in.

As for me, once my La Ferian husband Carl introduced me to the magic Valley, I stayed.

This morning the woodpecker trills comically in the mesquite outside my window. Doves offer their coy ventriloquism, and the mockingbird warms up his audacious repertoire. In a while, whiptail lizards will skitter across our sun-warmed patio and butterflies touch down on golden lantana.

Surely here is evidence that God has not saved all our soul delights for later in heaven.

— Jan Epton Seale

Black-tailed Jackrabbit

Amalgam

Light feeds on your ears:
sunsets, seashells, flamingoes,
cameos, tea roses, melons.

Chance plays in your eyes:
great glittery watchful marbles
at high stakes with hawk and coyote.

Olympiads run in your legs:
sprints, distances, high jumps,
and fine exhibitions of scratching.

Green Jay

Recipe for Ynca

1 batch of Mexican limes, still green
2 strips of race car detailing, bright yellow
1 baby's bib, midnight black
1 harlequin mask, midnight black
1 Caribbean ocean wave, cornflower blue
1 child's noisemaker

Divide the limes into two groups. Lay half aside to ripen and immediately fashion a bird's back with the bright green ones.

Add the yellow detailing to the outside of the tail. Waiting for the other limes to blush, mold a head with the ocean wave, allowing the wave to spill over into the face.

Now cover the eyes with the mask and apply the bib. Take the ripened limes and fashion a stout chest of light yellow.

Wire in the noisemaker, being careful to hook up all shrieks, caws, toots, and rattles.

When complete, stand back and admire.

Aloe Vera

Lover's Quarrel

You let me reach among your fleshy arms
to pluck out ravenous grass and leaves;
I try my best and yet you do me harm
with thorns like a nasty terrier's teeth.

Surprised for the hundredth time I view the blood
rising bright on its little path,
know what it means to be misunderstood,
and what must follow as aftermath.

I take a knife and circling you, with care
this time, I slice a flagging spear
and slather your green blood upon the tear.
I like to think we're now blood sisters, dear.

Argiope

Dinner Party

One morning, walking in brush,

you come upon a banquet spread:

fine silk-woven place mat,

silver of dew drops,

platter of stars,

napkins of rickrack.

Nearby stretches the chef,

calm in calisthenics,

awaiting a call

from the meat market.

Red-winged Blackbird

Hell's Angel

You black angel, you!
With those fiery wings—
matching front fenders,
scarlet hunks of macho—
dragging up and down
North America,
coming south for winter
like a circus,
getting refueled,
tanking up on rice,
corn, sorghum,
screaming, puffing up
bigger than Dixie,
claiming your women,
trying to make
things right with the locals
by your little charities:
eating harmful bugs
and weeds.

Purple Nightshade

Different

If only purple nightshade would upgrade,

agree to lead a more enchanting life,

it might be Milton's "glowing violet,"

or Wordsworth's "violet by a mossy stone."

But purple nightshade cannot put on airs,

though it gain a paradise or English wood.

It is content to grow out in a field,

with star-shaped purpleness its only good.

Little Blue Heron

Ironies

Like a thing of beauty may choose an ugly stick,

like the camera famishes forever the hunting bird,

like an immature Little Blue Heron is, of course, white—

In these things the world amuses itself with small laughter.

Queen's Wreath

Guest

Don't invite a vine to lunch
unless you can spend
the afternoon with it.
Leaping like a cat,
it will come in the back passage,
eat, curl itself into your lap.
While you doze, it goes exploring.
When you wake, its tendrils
have already signed a contract
with your fence.
                Pretty soon
you are answering it with "Yes, ma'am,"
and "Whatever you say, Your Highness."
You hit on a plan: "Queen for a Day"?

Before you know it, she's sprawled on her throne.
"Make that 'Queen for a Lifetime,' "
she says ever so sweetly.

Crested Caracara

Misplaced Royalty

There flew in a Crested Caracara

who wore on his head a tiara.

But he dined with the vulture

with manners *sans* culture.

'Twas clear his crown he did borrow.

Texas Horned Lizard

Hard to Come By

Little did we know—

chasing each other with you in hand,

or leading you about on a halter of string,

or scaring you, to squirt blood from your eyes,

or stroking your velvet belly,

or keeping you in a box on the porch—

little did we know

we'd have to show our grandchildren

pictures of you in a book,

so little do they know

about you.

Seagulls

Convention

Shadows of "M's" and "W's"

with solid breasts, keen eyes,

flat velvet colors, seagulls

always form a quorum.

In capital letters they vote

themselves favored spaces

between heaven and earth,

insist *they* are the rightful owners

of this particular day.

Black-throated Green Warbler

Memo to Make-up Dept.

General: This one to be contrastive: wild head/subtle body.

Wings: iron-gray w/ two white sidebars

Back: olive-green, a little mossy

Tail: figure something out between gray and green

Breast and belly: white but not too

Face: sunflower yellow, the more the better

P.S. When finished, leave black make-up bib on,
    with ties untied and trailing after.

Mesquite

In Praise of a Tree

If all we had were mesquites,
we'd still have roosts for birds,
holes for bugs, flowers for bees.

We'd still have furniture,
fence posts, and fires,
coffee and flour and jelly.

The past would still have
its wagon wheels, spokes,
gumdrops and glue.

The future would be sure
with places for kids to climb,
and rest for all in dappled shade.

Bobwhite Quail

Groundlings

Tramping fields, you may step
into a land mine,
a lift of feathered bodies
you thought was grass.

Later the pieces of motion will
return like a film run backwards,
to guard the eggs,
the family name: covey.

Bob White, if you ever were a man,
may you not have been a felon,
a no-good drifter, a liar, a cheat.
For your name rings clear
from the throats of little beasts
wound up with bright eyes, topknots,
ones who make a nest on the ground,
ignorant and brave.

Double-crested Cormorants

Conversation

—Look at it this way:
We could have been hatched in the Orient

      —and put to work catching fish all day.

—Rings around our necks—

      —Unable to swallow our catch.

—What a bummer!

      —As it is, we got work here in South Texas.

—Right! Posing in trees—

      —Mimicking the branches—

—Being bird nobility.

      —It's tough enough…

—but somebird's got to do it.

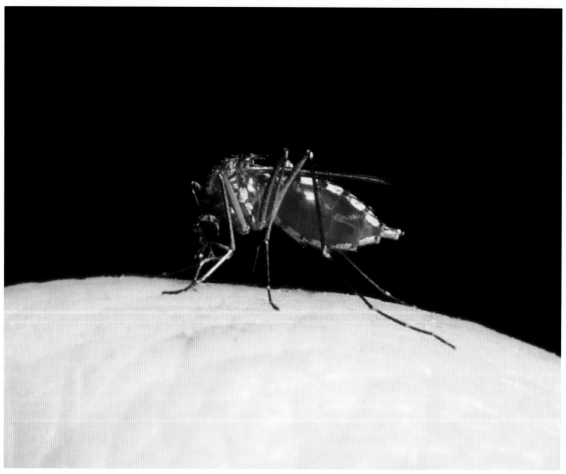

Mosquito

Eeeeeeeeee

With intention of a vampire,
whine of a Siren,
the mosquito pays you a call
at bed, easy chair, campfire.
She isn't about to mention
the millions she's done in
playing postman with fevers.
She'll not brag she can breed
in hydrochloric acid
(though she can),
not admit her own billions
donated to purple martins. No.

A true society lady,
she's just out for a little dessert,
having already had nectar today.
Just a smidgen of your life force.
There! See?
You didn't even notice.

Pyrruloxia

Lament

Many's the beginning birder
who's named you wrong:
female cardinal you're not!

What else can a bird do
to tout his unique specie-hood
than raise his topknot tall
and show his yellow parrot's beak?

Give us a name
we must pause to remember,
must practice, practice, practice.
Say you're a pyrruloxia.
Gracia!

Mountain laurel seeds

Off-balance

There's always something hanging around
to keep death from taking its due:
it wants to be sorrowful in brown,
airless, crusty, tumble-down.

But green will come along,
punctuate with an exclamation mark,
confuse the sadness, the inevitability.
Red too, dancing, shouting
like schoolchildren on their way home
from school, scuffling their feet
in the neat piles death has raked,
saying it's fun, fun, fun
to scatter the dull proper endings,
calling over their red shoulders
to get ready, that they'll be back
this route again tomorrow.

Ribbon Snake

After Rain

The green shoot growing,

the red tongue searching,

the black and yellow ribbon

gift-wrapping

a new world.

Cottontail Rabbit

Rabbitical Law

     I. Thou shalt not let any other animals run before me.

    II. Thou shalt not make graven images of me for greyhound races.

   III. Thou shalt not give the name of a rabbit to a hare.

   IV. Thou shalt not hunt me on Sundays.

    V. Thou shalt honor all our fathers and mothers.

  VI. Thou shalt not kill off my species.

 VII. Thou shalt not ask me not to commit adultery.

VIII. Thou shalt not ever try to steal up on me.

  IX. Thou shalt not tell lies about how much I eat.

   X. Thou shalt not covet my hide.

Monarch Butterflies

One Afternoon

A branch comes alive,
a dream-wrapped
stained-glass
cross-veined
tissue-papered
God joy.

Giant Toad

Admonition to Smart-aleck Dogs

There has been seen in this area
a large toad:
Brown,
with toad-like eyes,
a toady stare,
warts 'n' all.
He may be jumping.
He is eating the following:
flies, crickets, roaches,
small snakes, lizards.

You too must jump, but away.
You must run home yapping,
get down on your doggie haunches,
give thanks.
You were saved from this frog,
saved from his toxic sweat,
the milk of his back juice.

You did not kiss this frog.
This frog is not now,
nor ever will be
your prince.

Oleander

Overheard at a Bar

—Oleander was here.

　　　—Was she now?

—Yes, and she was covered in pink flowers.
　Everywhere. It was really something.

　　　—She can fix herself up pretty, all right.

—Tough too. Nothing phases her.

　　　—Yeah, but she's poison.

Collared Peccary

A Collared Peccary by any other name

would still be a javelina,
would deserve no respect—
some say, because
it has borrowed
the shape of pig
hide of wolf
hackles of porcupine
smell of skunk
bark of dog
rattle of snake.

So what's a poor javelina to do
to gain points in personal charm?

These are its favored things:
one elegant necklace of white,
two babies cherubic,
three curious toes on the hind feet,
and numberless prickly pear salads.

Greater Roadrunner of the Cuckoo family

Mr. Personality

I am anything but loco,
silly-willy, dumb-clucked.
I'm cuckoo like a stunt pilot,
a rodeo clown, a court jester.
Beep-beep! I'm a distance runner,
snake killer, faithful lover,
human's chum.

Call me any of my names:
chaparral, paisano, or
geococcyx californianus,
but know,
I'm not dumb as an ox,
I'm cuckoo like a fox.

Bougainvillea

First and Last Word

Bougainvillea,
it's hard not to see ya'!

Bewick's Wren

Emergency Measures

The tail pitches,
acts as though
it were bewitched
by a tailwind,
would take over,
become the head,
show the whole bird
who's boss.

The only way
to keep this
from happening
is to mount
a frantic concert.

Red-eared Slider

You Sweet Inscrutable You

Haven't changed much
Don't intend such

Love the sun
and when that's done

Don't go foodless
though you're toothless

Fishing's for you
and when that's through

It's forty winks
and time to think

what might have been,
but then again…

Prickly Pear Cactus

A Dozen Snapshots

I.
Where nothing else will grow,
and almost overnight,
big green hands.

II.
Who makes the choice—
this flower will be red,
this one yellow, this—orange?

III.
In the brush, I met a javelina.
Slurp! Crunch!
He could not be bothered,
so good was his salad of you.

IV.
You make robbery difficult
 with those spiny burglar bars.

V.
PRICKLY PEAR CONQUERS WORLD!

VI.
PRICKLY PEAR SAVES WORLD
FROM STARVATION!

VII.
If cactus wrens are so bird-brained,
how come we get stuck and they don't?

VIII.
Nopalitos! It could be the title
of a national anthem.

IX.
No rain? Never mind.
Here are magic pitchers.
Come, creatures. Sip.

X.
Are we certain these
simple punctures
are not
poisoned arrow tips?

XI.
The beauty and the beast,
one and the same.

XII.
You speak life—
dolor but *dulce.*

Mockingbird

Au Contraire

No wonder you were made gray.
Decent but not sensational.
Oh, larger and with better posture
than say, a humpbacked quail—
Sure, nice white military stripes.
We can't grant you
more pulchritude than that.

Singing? That's another story.
Your notes pour out
in rainbows, canyons, technicolor.
Rhythms? Rat-a-tat, ragtime, staccato.
Your songs like fractal geometry—
all over the place,
God doing riffs.

Green Anole

Still Life with Lizard

Little dragon—
Grand pooh-bah
of Lizardville—
Astride your citadel
you dream a dream,
wait to show
a passing lady
how brown skin
turns green,
how the throat
of a so-so lizard
can become,
on a macho male,
a sensational
red balloon.

Loggerhead Shrike

Warning to Small Critters

Killer bird reported in area—

Official name: Loggerhead Shrike

Alias: Butcher bird

Description: Lovely greys, distinct whites and blacks

Special markings: Wears black mask, sports hooked bill

Wanted for: Serial killing of beetles, grasshoppers, sparrows, lizards, frogs; ritualistically impales victim on thorns or other spiky objects

Last seen: In open country with scattered trees

If sighted: Run for cover!

Sea Ox-eye

Common

The sea ox-eye's a most happy plant,

who chose not to be elegant.

Poor drainage its temptation

and salt accumulation;

in marshes and swamps, rampant.

Mourning Dove

Hoo-Whoo

I am holy spirited,
a tail-and-wing meditation,
feathered calm.
Our kind
is royal blood:
Noah's pet,
Jesus' blessing.

Allow me one
light pleasure:
ventriloquism.
You hear
that cooing
over there?
Look up—
I'm here above!

Lantana

Bold

Something should like rocks,

and you do.

You play in the dirt.

You don't care

if anyone's looking

or not.

You're a calico dancer,

a fine loose woman.

You entertain quail.

You're happy as can be

out in nowhere.

Yellow Warbler

A Cautionary Tale

There was once a pair of yellow warblers who built a nest. But before they could place their eggs in it, a brown-headed cowbird came visiting and "accidentally" left her egg in their waiting crib.

"Tsee-tsee-tsee?" Mr. Warbler asked Mrs. Warbler, which translates, "Did you do that?"

"Gosh, no!" Mrs. Warbler said. "Remember? This happened once before."

"Yeah, and the bugger that hatched nearly ate us out of house and home."

The big egg was so....*there*. The Warblers hopped about excitedly until a plan came to their birdbrains. Bringing fresh twigs and other nesty things, they renovated their house, putting a new floor on top of the strange egg. The cowbird's egg was now in the basement.

But it happened again. The cowbird, way too busy to seek adequate childcare, laid an egg on the fresh first floor.

Now a warbler's brain is the size of an overgrown English pea, with little room for innovative ideas. So the couple fell back on their original plan. A second floor was added.

Each time the cowbird made an indiscrete deposit, the Warblers built a new floor over the outsized egg. Would you believe this happened three more times? Now Mr. and Mrs. Warbler had a five-storied nest with a basement.

"I've had it!" Mrs. Warbler chirped, and pronto! sat down on the fifth floor, like a contestant playing musical chairs.

The next time Mrs. Cowbird felt the need, she checked by, but it was too late for mooching. The Warblers incubated their eggs in their high-rise; a number of perfectly nice peepy little yellow warblers hatched.

And for years, the neighbors gossiped about the large strange fossilized eggs on the Warblers' lower floors.

The moral of this little story is, Don't put all your eggs in your first basket.

Pipevine Swallowtail Butterfly

Unsavory

Our eyes feeding on

your exquisite petticoats,

we thank whatever gods may be

for how un-delicious you are to birds.

All saturated with nasty pipevine,

you cause bird consternation,

detours, voluntary fasting—

bird zeal considerably bruised

at sight of your blacks and blues.

Anacahuita

Flowering Truth

Oh, the ordinariness of white!

How it doesn't as often bring goshes

or come-look-at-thises!

Still, there's the olive tree,

our only snow

floating down

with the grace of saints,

each white uncomplicated flower

a small angel,

a cousin to stars.

Golden-fronted Woodpecker

He's a...

ladder-backed   sunny-necked   red-crowned   white-bellied

chipper-tapping   chisel-wedging   rabble-rousing   driller-drumming

seed-eating   larva-licking   fly-flicking   nectar-sipping

wing-rowing   balance-beaming   joker-jeering   clamber-climber.

Palms

A Sanctuary of Palms

Step into a grove of palms.
Here you will be safe,
protected by silent old saints,
hushed by their prayers of endurance.

Cardinal

Three for Red

I.
Drinking him only with our eyes,
we find, after all, we had a hidden
thirst for his kind of red.

II.
If we all wore red all the time,
sparrows would make us swoon.

III.
Ever an omen, his churchman's coat
announces itself, bursts through gloom,
turns our dull day to miracle.

Opossum

A Dialog

Opinionated:

> We find you 'possums' pinkish noses
> upsetting, as are your well-formed toes, and
>
> there's the matter of your hair,
> which isn't quite from *here* to *there*.
>
> Your beady eyes and scary smile
> do anything except beguile;
>
> and as for that opposing thumb,
> we thought that *we* were number one.
>
> For such a slick-bald curling tail
> you really should be sent to jail.
>
> And do you think we are misled
> when you insist on playing dead?
>
> Some of us, without a blink,
> are hoping you'll become extinct.

Opossum:

> Just because I am unique,
> does it mean that I'm a freak?
>
> I eat lizards, rats, and mice,
> and if that is not deemed nice,
>
> I eat worms and garbage too—
> So don't put me in a stew!
>
> For those who want me out of sight,
> I'm a personage of night.
>
> For my pink nose, just look around—
> Not a few of yours abound.
>
> And for my prominent bald tail,
> replete with negative significance,
> I have to ask: Heads or tails?
> Is there a difference?
>
> And if my paws would seem like hands,
> and if my thumbs are quite opposing,
>
> this is something to endure
> without your prejudice exposing.
>
> Let me have my little pocket;
> let me play dead and grin;
>
> Oh, grant to me my 'possumhood,
> Opossuming's no sin!

Black-necked Stilts

Photo Op

They asked for an artsy pose,
mirror images, please,
one in sharp resolution,
the other in motion, fading.

They know they are beautiful,
oh yes, and just to make sure
the photographer was not tempted
to capture them in black and white,
they wore their red stockings.

Chachalaca

A Prayer

Dear God, This is to praise you
for your sense of humor.
Who would have thought
to make a bird the size of hawk,
the color of wren,
with feet of chicken
and grace of turkey,
and then, and then,
who would have had
the nerve to install
a combination
barking and crowing machine,
automatically set for dawn,
which, when the batteries are weak,
will cut back to chuckles and clucks?
Who but you, oh Lord?
Wow! and Amen.

Grapefruit

Short History of a Fruit

We see you hang like a gift
at Christmas, best décor of all.
Little sun, child's ball,
just right for the hand to lift.

First, in Polynesia, a pummelo,
then in West Indies, a shaddock
brought by a Capt. Shaddock,
no doubt a proud fellow.

"It tastes of grape in flavour,"
wrote John Lunan in 1814,
of this shaddock, stunning
his lips as he savoured.

With such a noble past,
and possessing juicy talent,
isn't the grapefruit due more praise,
in our yard or on our palate?

Roseate Skimmer

Airborne Fantasy

What if someone invented
a gossamer helicopter,

and what if each eye
could take a thousand
snapshots in all directions?

And what if it was an aircraft
that took off without effort,
glided, hovered, changed course,
like a flying saucer?

And what if it only made war
on mosquitoes?

What if it refueled its species
by love in tandem flight,
making us smile in envy?

What if we called it
Dragonfly?

Hackberry

Secret Keeper

A tree dies slow and full of secrets—
courtships of doves, nestlings,
the bobcat's soft pad, ants
in troop movements,
addictions of fungi,
indwelling of beetles,
deception of spiders.

Growing heavy
with its burden of tales,
and holding out to the
last possible moment,
it releases them

leaf upon leaf dropping.
Branches defy gravity,
preach on until
their arms collapse.
Roots finally curl,
glad to be underground.

Even in death, a tree
keeps up with its friends—
invites the woodpecker's gossip,
the vine's embrace.

Poinsettia

Trick

The *euphorbia pulcherrima*
is not much on blooms,
its tiny yellow blossoms
calling softly from the center,
pale yellow pitiful.

But oh those bracts!
Those laughing-out-loud
circling fires!
Those Hola Yoo-hoo starbursts!
Those gate-crashing splashes
of flower-thingies!

Sunset on the Circle

Subtropical

The southeast wind brings the smell of Gulf.
The orchid tree blushes a hundred blooms.
The cactus can't decide, pink or yellow,
all the while hiding its fruit like a girl.

I walk the circle, where the setting sun
and a cluster of palms plan a postcard.
It's a street with escape routes
but who would want them?

Someone needs to tell the woodpecker
it's evening, time to knock off.
A crowd of starlings is making
Susan's cottonwood shiver.

Homeward, I drag two dried fronds.
In the alley, a dead grackle,
still vain in his amethyst feathers
discovers me and grins.

I fold him in the fronds.
They are two of a kind,
a small funeral mound
against this excess life.

White-tailed Deer

Gone

Ears pricked, eyes staring round,
you hear motion, see sound,
and raising your white flag of tail,
arc away on a single bound.

No one knows exactly whom
your bleached behind addresses:
Fawns?— "Come along, dearies!"
Friends?— *"¡Vamonos, amigos!"*
Enemies?— "Don't even try!"

We are no further knowing
than the Aztecs who drew you
as the picture of goodbye.

Jan Epton Seale, a native Texan, writes and teaches writing from her home base in the Rio Grande Valley of Texas. Active in environmental work, she edited Creatures on the Edge, a Valley Land Fund pictorial. Her other writing includes The Wonder Is: New and Selected Poems 1974-2004. She and her husband Carl have three sons and three grandsons.

Ansen Seale, Jan's eldest son, lives and works in San Antonio with his wife Doerte and their son Luca. Ansen is an artist and photographer specializing in panoramic imagery. The work in this collection is the product of 25 years of visits to the Rio Grande Valley of Texas, his childhood home.